THE MACHIAVELLIAN MURDERS

AND HOMELESSNESS

BY

GEORGE B. HARPOLE

Authored by George B. Harpole
P.O. Box 1195
Clifton, CO - 81520

Printed by:
Createspace.com

Distributed by:
Amazon.com
and local bookstores

The Machiavellian Murders

Copyright © 2012 by George B. Harpole
P.O. Box 1195
Clifton, CO – 81520

Revised Printings in 2014 and 2016

All rights reserved, including those to reproduce, transmit or store this book or any part thereof in any form, without permission in writing from the author.

Some names have been fictionalized to protect the identity of the innocent.

ISBN – 9781480218598

~ ~ ~ ~ ~

For Marta

What's New?

This is a revised printing.

When this booklet was first published in 2012 the topics seemed to be taboo, but in 2016 internet search-hits have soared, e.g. "family court suicides" 21,400,000 hits, "family court corruption" 9,470,000 hits, "family court racketeering lawsuits" 65,000 hits, "homelessness" 15,700,000 hits, and more. At the same time, suicides and homelessness in the U.S. have increased. So, what can be done about it? Here, with this printing, I'm suggesting changes that would hopefully make our Family Courts more family friendly and less destructive. I hope you'll find these suggestions of interest, and that their implementations might help reduce Family Court related suicides and homelessness.

CONTENTS

Introduction	1
The Consequences of:	
Childhood Abandonment	7
Adult Separation	19
Judicial Discretions	39
Significance	60
Homelessness	63
A Program for Change	73
References	75

Introduction

My 34-year-old wife and mother of our two children committed suicide when our children were 7 and 8-years old. After 3-years of psychoanalysis and treatment, her depression and death were diagnosed to have been related to the traumatic experience of having her father disappear from her life when she was 3 years old. Thus, this story shows how long lasting and far reaching the effects of separation and divorce can have upon children.

Secondly, I look at my 1979-1985 divorce and realize how arbitrary a Family Court can be, and how they can collusively create ransoms so excessive as to cause a person to run, hide and sometimes even choose to suicide. I call the suicides Machiavellian murders because, as Niccolo Machiavelli advised his Prince in his book "The Prince," you must use someone else to be your "hatchet man" to do your dirty work, thus leaving you to look blameless.[4] Here our Family Courts have the power to give a person reasons to be their "hatchet" person, i.e. to kill themselves and leave the Family Court and others looking blameless.[3] The death of Tom Ball, in the later part of this booklet, is an example of what I call a Machiavellian murder.[3,4] Thus, many of our veteran suicides might be called Machiavellian murders. What do you think?

Of course not every person ravished by a Family Court kills himself or herself. Some stubbornly hang on to become homeless and hope for a better day. Currently our homeless populations appear to include a mix of men, women and children ranging from some 600,000 for the chronically homeless to as many as 3.5-million when counting those homeless for less than a year.[8]

I came from a family laced with three generations of Lawyers, two of them licensed to practice before the Supreme Court of the United States. This strongly influenced me. I would trust any one of them with my life and proudly witnessed the fairness and level of ethical consideration they gave to others. But one is naive to believe all who are licensed to be Judges or practice law are fair-minded or ethical. Of recent years we discovered pedophiles in our religious and educational circles. So who's to say we don't have pedophiles and sadism in our Family Court systems?

We should hope the system has a self-cleaning mechanism by way of those Offices of Professional Responsibility to where you can send complaints about deviations from the rule of law. If justified, give it a try. But don't be surprised to have a reply declaring, "There is _utterly_ no evidence to support your complaint." Here the word "_utterly_" seems to have some fraternal significance.

In any case, the deviates in our Family Courts appear to represent only a small percent of the total, but who appear to be well protected by their brethren. Consequently, the culprits might collectively represent one of the largest and most sophisticated crime organizations in the United States - where they are typically protected by law from criminal and civil prosecutions to run their 50-billion dollar per year business.[6,7]

Family Courts do not offer litigants a choice for jury judgments. In the Family Court, the Judge is the law, and Lawyers have little fear of making false statements, to present false evidence, to insult, or to make inflammatory or slanderous accusations. For instance: Her Lawyer writes, "And, he now wants to throw her away like an old pair of shoes!"

He says: "He should try walking in those shoes!"

Her Lawyer says: "I'm going to come across the table and bust you in the mouth!"

Those were recorded and billed exchanges that often go on-and-on in the Family Court, and cost hundreds of dollars per billing hour. Isn't it interesting that these cakewalks can only be billed with a Judges approval? You just wanted a divorce and the **Family Court** requires you to listen to and pay for these sideshows?

On the other hand, just a couple of months ago, a friend of mine went into a Family Court Pro-se (without an Attorney) and pointed out his legal bases to support his request regarding a child custody issue. Ha? Whatever, the Judge found him in contempt of court and remanded him to jail for 30-days. So check the Internet for suicide and homelessness, and the "Divorce Corp." DVD and look to see what's happening.[1,2,3,6,7,8]

Judges, judicious or vicious, have powers we need to be fearful of. According to my information a Family Court Judge can tag you for contempt for little or no reason and have you locked up in a county jail for up to a year – without a jury to find you guilty or not guilty of any specific charges.

For ordinary people, like you and me, we are well advised to be humble and respectful before even the lowliest of Judges. So, don't piss the Judge off. And be forewarned that going pro-se (being your own lawyer) can in-and-of-itself be a reason for a Family Court Judge to put you away. This shouldn't be, but is.

So be respectful of the Judge. And don't hesitate to beg for mercy.

There is good news. There is hope for making our Family Courts more family friendly, and in such spirit a seven-step program for reducing our national rates and numbers for suicides and homelessness is offered in the last Chapter of this booklet, titled "A Program for Change" starting on page 73.

Okay?

Childhood Abandonment

Thirty four year old Marta serves as an example of the lasting impact parental abandonment can have upon a child that can carry forth with them disastrously into their adult life.

Professionally described, childhood abandonment can leave a lifetime of inner mourning and depression referred to as a **Childhood Abandonment Stress Disorder.** This stress disorder (SD) is where the "inner critic" of a child associates feelings of shame and self-hate for imagined imperfections as reasons for why they were abandoned. Thus, the victim is driven towards perfectionism by feelings of endangerment, fear, self-hate, and self-disgust that originated from the childhood abandonment experience (Pete Walker, M.A., MFT).

Thus, these disorders can understandably lead to adulthood depression and suicide, like for Marta, who was my wife and mother of our two children. In her case, a divorce suddenly eliminated her father from her life. We don't know why, i.e. if this happened because of a Court decree or if he disappeared simply to avoid his financial responsibilities. He did disappear suddenly, and nobody could ever tell Marta or her brother why. Marta was 3-years old when this happened. Her eventual resolution was to suicide at the age of 34, leaving her two children in much the same way as she was abandoned.

Our local newspaper published:

"Marta Blair Harpole passed away unexpectedly Tuesday evening in Walnut Creek, California. She was born in Missoula, Montana where she graduated from High School and attended her first year of college at the University of Montana. Before becoming married to George Harpole in

1959 she was the manager of a restaurant in Missoula, Montana.

George's job moved them to Chicago in 1960 where their two sons were born. In 1964 George's job moved them to the San Francisco bay area where they bought a house in Walnut Creek.

Marta's love was for her children and husband, and for family celebrations with parents, brother and in-laws as well as for socializing with the many working associates of George's, and her friends and neighbors who would drop by for a cup of coffee. She was also known for her love of flowers, and for her garden. Marta is survived by her mother Bea Blair, brother John Blair; and, husband George and son's Gene (8 years old) and Blair (7 years old).

Services will be held at Hull's Walnut Creek Chapel on Saturday, August 30, 1969."

- - - - # - - - -

What Marta's obituary didn't say was that maybe Marta died as a consequence of what Dr. Lewellen Jones called a "psychotic depressive reaction," or what we now call a "Post Traumatic Stress Disorder," or a "Childhood Abandonment Stress

Disorder." Their father Carl Blair disappeared when Marta was 3 years old and her brother 6. As adults, they could never think about his disappearance without feeling bewilderment, sadness, and anger. They knew their parents divorced, but Marta could never remember anything said about why she never saw or heard from him again - even after much searching by both Marta and her brother on into and through their adult life.

Apart from Marta's curiosity about what might have happened to her father, or where he might be, the fortunes of life were good to her. I had a good job with Potlatch Forest, Inc. (PFI) and my recent promotion moved us from Chicago to Walnut Creek, California where we found a house close to an elementary school and a neighborhood swimming pool. We felt lucky and secure. We were in a trendy neighborhood where Marta began driving our second car, an attractive Ford convertible. We adopted a cat and dog, and our boys were now 3 and 4 years old and healthy. What more could we ask for?

Without any identifiable reason Marta began feeling anxious. She consulted with her doctor about her concern. Having 3 and 4 year old boys could be the explanation, for which her Doctor gave her a prescription for Librium, an antianxiety drug, with instructions to take one 5-mg capsule each day.

The prescription worked, but Marta wasn't the same. She smoked more and drank more coffee, and seemed apprehensive. In response, I made a job change to be closer to home, i.e. to work at the Forest Service's Pacific Southwest Forest and Range Experiment Station (PSW) located in Berkeley. As a Conservation Economist there would be little to no travel with a 40-hour workweek. The one way commute from home was reduced from about 1-hour to San Francisco, on a good day, to about 20-minutes for Berkeley.

Things still did not go well. Marta's Doctor increased her daily dosage of Librium to 10-mg. She said she was still uncomfortable and said she was afraid she might lose her temper and do harm to our boys. The boys were healthy and active, and pretty normal for their age. They had made neighborhood friends and sometimes seemed to run wild, but never into anything for us to be seriously concerned about.

In the meantime I worried about Marta's concern. Shortly after Marta started expressing her concerns, her Doctor increased her Librium prescription again, from 10-mg per day to 25-mg.

Then, I came home from work on a Friday that was to be a Thanksgiving weekend. Marta appeared to be asleep on the couch, but was unconscious from taking an entire 30-day supply of 25-mg Librium capsules. I got her to the Contra Costa Emergency medical center and told them what she had done. This was her first attempt at suicide. They kept her for several days, and then the psychological assessments and family counseling began. The roadway was all down hill, with 3 more suicide attempts before her last.

Her doctor, Dr. Lewellen Jones at the Napa State Mental Hospital in Napa diagnosed her as having a psychotic depressive reaction, i.e. a psychological aberration caused by a subdued early life experience of abandonment. During her third year of depression (January 24, 1969) Dr. L. Jones wrote: " . . . with whatever improvement we might find she will probably never be forever free from this kind of depression." Today, the doctors call her depressive reaction a Post Traumatic or Childhood Abandonment Stress Disorder (SD) - a potentially debilitating anxiety disorder initiated by a traumatic experience much like for those losing husbands, wives, relatives and friends in the New York Twin Towers terrorist attack of September 11, 2001, or perhaps for a child losing a parent by way of a Family Court child custody decision.

Marta fooled everyone except her Doctors. Like others, I saw Marta as thinking, talking and acting rationally and normal. At the same time, she started looking and acting tired. Then, out of the blue, she would attempt to suicide. She would tell me she didn't know why, and through her tears she would tell me she loved the boys and me and everything was okay. She didn't know why, but she just seemed to want to die. Her psychologist thought the trigger was when Gene and Blair reached the same age as when she and her brother experienced the loss of their father. She had been 3 years old, and now Gene was 4 and Blair 3 when she started having her first remorseful feelings.

What could I do? No one seemed to understand so we just tried to hide the situation as best as we could. I thought maybe we needed more family time together. So, in August of 1969 I arranged for us to take a 10-day vacation to Montana and visit Marta's mother. I put camping equipment in the trunk of Marta's 1957 Ford Fairlane convertible and we took off for a carefree vacation with the boys. They were then 7 and 8 years old. Every day was a sunny day and we enjoyed the drive from California in Marta's convertible with the top down. When we got to Missoula we found Bea, Marta's mother, in good health and good spirits. We had a good visit by proudly showing off our children Gene and Blair to their Grandmother.

This seemed like a carefree "family together" vacation. I felt good about Marta. She seemed to be having a good time. On the last leg of our drive going home we were on highway 80 headed towards Sacramento, the weather was clear and warm, and a full moon was high overhead. I was tired and Marta had been dozing. The boys were asleep in the back seat. I asked Marta if she would drive so I could take a break. She agreed, so I pulled over on the shoulder and switched with her.

I got comfortable and waited for her to pull out. She delayed a bit to see me get comfortable, and seemingly to check the oncoming traffic from behind. Suddenly, she hit the gas!

An 18-wheeler had been coming in the passing lane to give us clearance, but Marta accelerated directly towards the side of the speeding truck-trailer. I screamed, "No! No!" I grabbed the steering wheel to steer us away from the truck.

The truck went by. Marta then pulled the car to the right and slowed to a stop on the shoulder. The boys were still asleep in the back seat. All I could say was: "Please! No." All the time I was wondering how I could cool the situation, to make it not to have happened. We talked. She finally said she was okay to let her continue driving. I said okay and got back into a comfortable position on the passenger side.

I might have looked relaxed, pretending what had happened hadn't really happened. My God! What if we had run into the side of that truck? We didn't wear safety belts in those days, and we were in a convertible with the top down.

That was years ago, but my hands sweat even as I write about this now.

We arrived home after midnight and put the kids in bed. We woke up somewhat late in the morning. The kids were the first to stir. It was Sunday. We got the car unpacked, and everything back in place. I took the next day off, Monday, to help get clothes through the laundry, wash Marta's car and to do whatever else needed to be done to make us feel like we were home again.

Yes, we were home again. Thus I went back to work on Tuesday, riding with our car pool. The workday went by fast and I looked forward to coming home. When I got home Marta's car was gone and the boys were on the couch watching TV. It was about 6 p.m. I asked where their mother was. Gene said she left saying she was going to the grocery store. After a moment, he looked up at me and said, "She said she loved us. But, she had tears in her eyes."

I was struck with panic. All my inside alarms went off. She's been gone too long to just go to the grocery store. Maybe she went back to the Contra Costa Clinic. I called. She wasn't there. I called Dr. L. Jones's emergency number in Napa. I got him on the telephone almost immediately. He said he hadn't had any contact with her, but said I should call the police. I did, and told them she had a tendency to be suicidal.

At about 9:00 p.m. a police officer called who told me they thought they had found her and I should come to a local funeral parlor where they had taken her body. She had identification on her so they knew who she was, but wanted me to identify her.

It was Marta. Thirty-four years old, good physical health, married, two healthy children ages now 7 and 8. She died of a gunshot wound to her head. Her body was found at 7:40 p.m. August 26th 1969 in a gas station restroom.

What happened? Was this because of a long ago child custody decision, or abandonment by way of an irresponsible father? Was the Librium helping her, or did it bring her into doing this? Who's fault was this? Was this an inevitable outcome regardless of the treatment she could have had?

My parents, brother, sister and many friends attended Marta's funeral. Gene and Blair were not there. I left them with a neighbor. I could not share their Mother's funeral with them. When it came time for a eulogy I could only say, "Goodbye Marta." I choked and sat down. Nobody else said anything. Our friends and family mingled, showed tears, expressed condolences and went home.

During the next two weeks of darkness and suspension, a 14-year old boy around the corner from us shot himself in the head, the next-door just divorced 50-year-old woman drove to the bay bridge and jumped to her death. A few weeks later the father with six children who lived across the street died of a heart attack, and the mother of Gene and Blair's good friend (three houses away) died of a massive thrombosis.

These were neighbors who knew Marta, which either emphasize a series of coincidences, or the far-reaching precipitous effects childhood traumas of one can have on others.

A few years later after Marta's death, with her Father on his deathbed, he called Marta's brother to let him know where he was and some of his history since leaving the family. He never explained why he totally disappeared from their lives for so many years.

The Consequences of <u>Adult Separation</u>

- - - - # - - - -

<u>**Adult Separation Anxiety Disorder**</u> has been reportedly an unrecognised mental disorder until the late 1990's (Wikipeia: Separation anxiety disorder). The symptoms include:

• Extreme anxiety and fear when separated from major attachment figures. This anxiety may manifest in the form of full-blown panic attacks.

• Avoidance of being alone.

• Fears that something bad will happen to their loved ones.

Two years after Marta's death, in 1971, I met Anna in Hawaii on an elevator. I was on my way with sons Gene and Blair to attend a luau on Waikiki beach in Oahu, Hawaii. Anna was a strikingly attractive well-dressed dark haired young woman. She was short, about 5-ft 4-in tall, with a personable presence. She had sparkling eyes and a smile to match. When she looked at my boys I acknowledged her by introducing her to Gene and Blair. She asked them where they were going in a clear voice with a slight accent. Gene told her we were going to a luau. I followed his comment by telling her we were going to a luau that would mark the beginning of a three islands 5-day tour. I told her our tour would cover the island where we were, the island of Oahu, then on to the Big Island of Hawaii, and finish on the Garden Island of Kauai.

Her eyes brightened. She said she was on the same 5-day tour, and was also on her way to the luau. She indicated she was alone, so I suggested she might join us. She smiled. I thought she was very pretty. It was an interesting evening with an introduction to a variety of Hawaiian foods, Polynesian hula dancing, and music for entertainment.

I told Anna I was widowed and our island tour was to help take Gene and Blair beyond the loss of their mother. She reciprocated by telling me much about herself. I then began to wonder if this was a chance in a million meetings, a supernatural encounter, or maybe a meeting arranged by God. No matter, we both seemed okay to explore our contact. What I learned about Anna over the next few days was fascinating.

Anna was charming, and seemed open and honest in telling me she had been in the United States for only three years, coming from Tehran, Iran to be with her family, who had started emigrating to the U.S. six years earlier. Her father, Michael had been in the import-export business in Tehran and had a heart attack and passed away only a year after being in the United States, leaving her mother with her two brothers and two sisters. Each had come to the United States one after the other, as they were able to obtain exit visas from Tehran. She explained it wasn't easy to get an exit visa, and the visa's came only by way of graciously tendering money in unmarked envelopes to the people you asked as to where you stood for your visa. She smiled and said all her family had to do the same. The Zurian's had enough money to pay the bribes, and to buy real estate in the Modesto and San Francisco areas of California after they came to the United States.

Anna was the youngest in the family, and last to leave Tehran. The reasons for this surfaced later.

She explained how her mother and grandmother had lived in Turkey in the early 1900's, and how they had fled to Iran when the Islamic mullahs of Turkey sought to solve the Ottoman Empire's economic problems by confiscating the property and wealth of their Christian populations. The Islamic crusade was then underwritten by the declaration that one would be favored in the eyes of Allah if they should kill a Christian. Here history shows the Armenian's to be the first to follow the words of Jesus Christ and call themselves Christians. The Assyrians, also of Bablonic decent, followed in the footsteps of the Armenians to call themselves Christians. Both were minority groups in the Middle East and thus fled largely into Iran where they thought they would be safe. Many were killed on the road while trying to flee Turkey, and those too old and weak to walk were left to die – like Anna's grandmother.

Historic records indicate some 3-million of a total of 6-million Armenians were killed during those years of the Ottoman Empire's Islamic purge of Christians (1915-1923). This religiously sanctioned slaughter did little to nothing to solve the economic problems of the Ottoman Empire, and lost the Empire's respect and trust in all middle eastern and European trade circles.

Anna's mother, Yome, after almost hysterically leaving her mother behind on a dirt road in Turkey took refuge with an Assyrian family in the northern Iranian city of Hamedan. There she married a member of the Zurian family – Michael Zurian. Yome and Michael later moved to Tehran where Michael made a living in the import-export business - especially in the trade of the Persian carpets produced in Iran. Some of the hand woven silk carpets could be sold for prices greater than the price for a new house.

Michael and Yome raised their family of five children in Tehran, but with the trepidations prudently held by minority groups of Jewish and Christian faith. Most fearful were the days during the Islamic celebrations of Ramadan when laws against doing harm to the so-called infidels seemed to be suspended or ignored.

What an education. I was raised in California with many years in Idaho, Montana and Chicago, Illinois where racial mixes seemed to be from all parts of the world – except from the Middle East. I saw some racial unfairness and discrimination, but nothing like what Anna described. They were survivors, and escaped to the United States primarily through doorways opened by way of bribery and whatever else it took. I wondered how much their desperation might have matched my ancestor's of 10 generations ago when they fled from the 30-year war in Germany to come to the United States in 1774.

On the lighter side, we enjoyed our tour of the Hawaiian Islands by mixing with and meeting other people. On one of the roadside stops on the lee side of the Big Island of Hawaii we were allowed to explore cave entrances to volcanic tubes that ran out towards the ocean where Gene and Blair quickly got lost exploring the nooks and crannies of the tubes. When it came time to board the bus to continue our tour they were nowhere to be found. I was concerned because we were warned about possible drops and pits in the volcanic tubes – just the thing explorative small fry might like to discover. Yes, I was concerned, but it was Anna who sounded the alarm. In a minute she had our busload of tourists back into the tubes looking for them. Then, they reappeared. They'd mixed in with people from another tour who had flashlights to follow them into the deeper recesses of the tubes. They explained they couldn't come back on their own because they didn't have any flashlights. We got them on our bus and continued our tour.

Anna said she was just out of a divorce from a marriage that only lasted a short time and was employed as a reconciliation clerk at a brokerage house in San Francisco. She said she could speak five languages, e.g. Farsi (Persian), Armenian, Assyrian, French and English.

We returned to the Bay Area where Anna lived with her mother Yome and brother Bobby in San Francisco. I lived in Walnut Creek - approximately 25-miles from Anna. Being a working single parent kept me busy, thus I didn't see Anna more than once or twice a month - for dinner or for something we could do together with my boys. These visits were always comfortable, and I found both her mother Yome and brother Bobby to also be pleasant to visit with.

As time went by, I became acquainted with her other brother and two sisters. I liked the Azurian family, and felt a special fondness for Anna. She was good for us, and she was something special to me by this time.

MARRIAGE

In 1973 my supervisor at the Forest Service's Pacific Southwest Forest and Range Experiment Station (PSW) in Berkeley advised they would like to have me transfer to Madison Wisconsin to work at the Forest Service's Forest Products Laboratory in a new position where I would perform assessments of the commercial potentials for the new products and processing systems being developed there. It was a pioneering assignment – never before being done at the Forest Products Laboratory. I had prior experience with these kinds of assignments while working for PFI, so welcomed the opportunity. With all things considered, I liked the idea of moving away from where we had suffered the loss of Marta, and thought having a new place to live with a new job assignment would give us a new life to help us move ahead.

By this time I was well acquainted with Anna's family. Anna had also had a chance to become acquainted with my mother and father who lived in Clear Lake, California. At this point I was careful about what I told her about my forthcoming transfer to the FPL in Madison – telling her I was actually working for the FPL while keeping an office at the PSW station in Berkeley for at least the next year. Bit by bit I fed her the prospects, and then asked if she would marry me. "Me," of course, included Gene and Blair.

In response to my proposal, Anna said she would have to think about it. I knew she meant she would discuss my proposal with her mother, brothers and sisters. Of course, I couldn't imagine pursuing a marriage with her unless she had approval from her family.

A few days later Anna said "yes." We were married June 2, 1974 and left the children with my parents at Clearlake, California while we ventured to Madison, Wisconsin. At the end of June 1974 we chose to buy a house that was still under construction. I made the down payment with proceeds from the sale of my house in Walnut Creek, California. Anna then worked with the builder in modifying the floor plan for the house, in specifying paint colors, selecting high quality carpeting, modifying the design of the kitchen to include a double oven, and on through each and every detail of the house. She was so agreeable in the way she worked with the builder, he and his family became our close friends. Finally, I arranged to have Gene and Blair fly to Madison so we could move into our beautiful new home located in Middleton, Wisconsin just as their fall school session began. For me, the FPL was only a 15-minute drive away, but I still arranged for a car pool ride with a fellow employee who lived only a few blocks away.

Life was good. Anna was happy, Gene and Blair were happy, and I found my work at the Forest Products Laboratory (FPL) interesting. I moved rapidly from a GS-12 level of research employment to a mid-level GS-14.

I give much credit to Anna for those good years. Anna's spirit and accomplishments were uplifting and generated a great feeling of love for her. Part of the joy we found was from having her being a fantastic cook. She brought with her Middle Eastern traditional dishes of sabzi palo (long grain rice with vegetables and herbs), and servings of dolma and sarma (ground meat or rice recipes wrapped in grape leaves), with baklava served as a treat for special occasions. We loved Anna.

We watched Gene and Blair grow and prosper in their new school environment. They made many friends who visited in and out of our house, and to their houses. I was proud of them, and proud of Anna for developing such a good bond with both of them. Yes, Anna was our salvation.

The Downturn

Things started to change in October of 1977.

Someone called Anna saying they were with the U.S. Assyrian American Club (AAC) in California telling her the Shah of Iran was flying to the United States to meet with Jimmy Carter in Washington, D.C. on November 13th. This was at a time of strong anti-Shah feelings in Iran with violent student rioting in Tehran. Because of the Shah's long standing position for protecting the minority Jewish and Christian groups in Iran the AAC was recruiting as many Assyrians and Armenians as possible to go to Washington, D.C. to show support for the Shah while he was there. To do so, they were offering to pay costs for a round trip flight and a hotel room, plus $200 to anyone who would make an appearance in support of the Shah. She told him she would like to go but would have to let him know. She checked with her brother Bobby in San Francisco who said he was going. I couldn't go because I had a prior travel commitment. And, although Anna's brother Bobby was going, I told her I didn't think she should go because I thought there might be violence like already reported from Iran. Her brother Bobby went, but Anna and I did not.

As we now know, the Shah Reza Pahlavi was on his last legs as the ruler of Iran. The Shah's constitutional government collapsed following widespread "student" type uprisings during the years of 1978 and 1979, having his government replaced by an Islamic Republic government led by Ayatollah Khomeini. (View the 2012 movie "Argo" for a peek into this phase of Iran's history.) Thus, the Shah left Iran in January of 1979 to begin a life in exile – dying from cancer on July 27, 1980 while living in Egypt.

In 1978 Anna was still a citizen of Iran and still corresponded with friends who lived in Tehran. She was concerned for her friends about what was happening in Iran. Minority groups were in danger, as well as any supporters of the Shah's regime. It is well known that the members and supporters of a prior regime, once overthrown, would be threatened with execution - especially if overthrown by an Islamic dominated government. I didn't know how serious this seemed to her. She was still an official citizen of Iran; hence I encourage her to file an application for U.S. citizenship. I had to encourage her several times before she did. Her hesitation made me wonder. Did she think she could actually fail the fairly simple exam given on U.S. history, or perhaps for something I didn't know? The required information was given to her to study, and I chided her with the thought the most difficult question on the exam would probably be like: "What color is the white house?" Ha!

Anna studied the given information related to the history and constitution of the United States, filed her application, successfully took her examination, and in the early part of 1978 stood with others before a magistrate to swear her allegiance of loyalty to the United States of America.

What I didn't know then I learned later, that while in her 20s Anna had married a Moslem who was the son of a doctor to the Shah. Anna gave birth to a son who would be about the same age as Gene or Blair. But, as anti-Shah sentiments increased in the late 1960's her Moslem husband encouraged her to leave Tehran to live with her family in San Francisco – and maybe, or maybe not, follow with their son later. As political unrest in Iran increased, it became impossible for him to leave – wherewith Anna apparently thought she would never see him or her son again. This seemed to explain the regular correspondences from Tehran containing at least 4 tissue paper pages covered with Persian Farsi writing. I couldn't read the writing, and Anna never had much to say about what the letters said – except to say they were from a friend who still lived in Tehran. She always acted a bit somber from reading the letters. I felt like there was something important she wasn't telling me, but accepted her comment that they were from a dear friend still living in Tehran.

Later, in the mid-1980's an anonymous person told me, on the fall of the Shah's regime, that Anna had been married to a Moslem and given birth to a boy who would be about the same age as Gene or Blair. And, that her father-in-law had been a doctor to the Shah and ordered to be executed. However, while waiting for his execution he suffered a heart attack. By Islamic law, Allah had spared his life and therefore he was not to be executed. He was allowed to continue to practice medicine, but forbidden to gain any profit by way of his practice.

I've never been able to find out what happened to Anna's husband, or her son, but I can clearly understand her escalating levels of anxiety because they coincided so closely to the change in political control in Iran, i.e. from the Shah's constitutional government to Islamic law – where the defeated government officials and supporters were rounded up and summarily executed. In the meantime, Anna had developed an explosive temperament that couldn't be explained. At first I thought it might be a side effect from the medications she was taking. But I didn't know and she couldn't tell me.

With so much that had been so good for us it was now disappearing. I was wondering what was wrong. I loved Anna as well as feeling greatly indebted to her. She had become the cornerstone of my life, as well as for Gene and Blair's. It was now 1980 and both Gene and Blair were out of high school, out of the house and had good apprentice level oilfield employment in Wyoming. Hence, we were proud of them, but Anna was irrationally irritable and subject to becoming confrontational with anybody she came in contact with. With this, her temper cost us friendships we had with other emigrant Armenians in the Madison area. They were dismayed and alienated by her outbursts, and I was unable to explain what was wrong. I got her to visit a family counselor with me in hopes of finding out what was wrong, and what we might do to make life more carefree now that the boys were out of the house and doing well.

Then, on her coming home from running errands on a Saturday afternoon, I heard the two-car garage door open, and the house shuddered. She had hit the side of the garage entrance with damage to her car as well as to the house. She came in the house but not walking or acting normally. When I asked what happened, she flew into a rage about my being demeaning, I never ever took her anywhere, nobody was nice to her, etc., etc.!

When I asked her what was going on she came directly to me, all 5-ft 4-in, shouting there was nothing wrong with her and everything was wrong with me, etc. etc.! She didn't smell of alcohol, and was never prone to have more than one or two drinks at a time. I was puzzled. Was it a medication?

I hastened to exit the house through the sliding glass door for the back yard. I was thinking we were free to travel whenever we wanted, and did, e.g. New Orleans, the Bahamas, Memphis as well as her going with me on business trips. And, she made one or two trips back to California to visit with her family every year. Things didn't add up. I couldn't imagine what was wrong? Is this a panic attack, or a problem with her medications?

Anna's anxieties and discontent lingered, and were unexplainable. We continued family counseling. In fact, when the first Psychiatrist didn't seem to get us anywhere I got Anna to go with me to see a second Psychiatrist. Both Psychiatrists explained to me privately that Anna seemed to have excessively strong ties to her family, who lived in California, and that those ties had not diminished. They both suggested I should consider a separation or divorce to allow her to settle whatever it was she was having problems with. I was surprised because I always thought family counselors never suggested divorce as a way to resolve a marital problem, but they did. I think they must have seen something I couldn't.

However, having lost my first wife by way of her becoming depressed, and then committing suicide, I couldn't bear to think the same kind of incomprehensible situation was happening again. I was heartbroken. What was I doing? What could I do? I knew I couldn't take her down the same pathway Marta had traveled. I knew I had to let her go, if she needed to go.

I talked to her about separation, and in January of 1983 I filed for a divorce. I told her she should let me know if she really didn't want the divorce, and if she wanted to stay in the marriage we must get to the bottom of her discontentment. I knew something was going on. I let her know this was hard but seemed to be what our family counselors thought would be best.

As for a divorce, I agreed with my Attorney we could sell the house with any other assets we had in Madison, and each take half. Even though I made the original down payment on the house with non-marital money. I also agreed Anna could take whatever furniture and personal property she wanted, and I would help her with her costs for moving back to California along with temporary support.

My Attorney thought we should be able to reach a divorce agreement in a few weeks and be on our way. He said we just needed to sell the house and have an accountant add up the proceeds with our bank accounts and divide by two. I was agreeable and hoped for an amicable divorce.

I talked to Anna about how we could do this, and she could be home in California again. I even gave her the names of a couple of reputable Lawyers she might contact. Anna seemed sad, but agreeable to the ideas we discussed. There didn't seem to be any reason for complications because Anna had interest in income producing properties in California (presumably inherited by way of her father), and a desire to return to live with her family in California. (I didn't then know about her Iranian husband and son.) But, Anna found her way into the McManus Law Offices and Angela Bartell's courtroom of Madison, Wisconsin - from which there was no escape for the next 5 years.

At one time one of my Attorney's said: "It could have been worse."

Above all, the Lawyers seemed happy.

Judicial Discretions

I filed for divorce - 1/11/1983

Our divorce could have gone quickly and quietly - a couple of country Lawyers and an accountant could add the marital assets up, and divide by two. We could call everything we had in Wisconsin marital and not quibble about Anna's real estate in California where she seemed to want to return. She seemed to be agreeable with these ideas. Thus, we could have settled everything in a couple of months or less, but for matters of judicial discretions it took 5 years.

The McManus Law Office and Judge Angela Bartell of Madison, Wisconsin stepped in – first having me leave my house to live in a low-rent apartment with a card table, folding chairs and sleeping bag. I had a wardrobe of clothes and moved my gun collection and camping equipment over to my hunting buddies house. Then, Anna's Attorney, Robert Burr, declared I presented a threat for violence; and I should be treated accordingly.

For billable activities, Robert Burr ran a crusade of delay, meaningless court hearings, and unnecessary employment intrusions that had little to do with our petition for a divorce. I wrote a letter to the Judge objecting to what I regarded as Robert Burr's billings for harassment activities that seemingly had nothing to do with us getting a divorce. The Judge never responded and Attorney Robert Burr continued doing his thing.

Then the Judge ordered us to visit a family counselor. This order ignored the fact we had already spent two years with two different family counselors who suggested we should separate or divorce to allow Anna to find her emotional needs with her family in California. Another needless time delay and expense, possibly to benefit a friend of the court.

Because my Attorney specialized in real estate and probate law, we agreed I should get an experienced divorce Attorney. Hence, I paid a retainer to James Cassidy, a Madison Attorney who had a good reputation and had served as a County Court Commissioner. I thought he would know all of the in's and out's of the divorce process. Also, he had served in the U.S. Marine Corp., which proved to be of value when Anna's Attorney Robert O. Burr threatened to "bust" me in the mouth during one of our court hearings, and by stepping in when tough looking Attorney (Denis Seig), approximately 6-ft tall and 180-lbs, presented a potential hands-on incident in the foyer of the Federal Bankruptcy Court just prior to the preliminary hearing for my petition for bankruptcy. This would have canceled my petition for bankruptcy by preventing me from appearing in court - as required.

There were several attempts to draw me into behavior that could label me as a violent person. Apparently there was no such concern for the perpetrators. For Attorney Robert Burr, complaints to the Wisconsin State Board of Professional Responsibility brought a response that there was "utterly" no evidence of his physically threatening me in the courtroom, even though Robert Burr blatantly admitted in writing that he had. I was impressed by the "utterly no evidence" response. It seemed to be an expression happily used in responses from the Wisconsin Board of Professional Responsibility.

As for violence, Robert Burr was a little guy, maybe 5-ft 6-inches tall and 160-lbs. He didn't look like a fighter, but one never knows. He wore shoes with two or three inch lifts. However, a reliable source told me he had cleverly angered two male spouses to a degree to where they murdered his female clients. To my way of thinking, this is another kind of Machiavellian murder. I could see he'd been working on me too, but thought somebody should tell him he was wasting our time.

Thinking of Robert Burr, I looked to the Internet to find figures as to the number of Wisconsin Attorney's found guilty of acting unethically, but couldn't find anything. This seemed to be explained by a Journal Sentinel Watchdog report by Cary Spivak and Ben Poston (Jan. 29, 2011) that said the Attorney discipline system operates largely behind closed doors where it can favor Lawyers at the expense of their clients.

At one hearing, Lawyer Dennis Seig (McManus Law firm) leveled a contempt charge against me. I demonstrated he lied by way of evidence he had just submitted. Judge Bartell pressed Dennis Seig as to whether or not he really wanted to enter his false charge into the court's record. He finally realized his error and withdrew his charge, and was forgiven by the court. Later, on another case, the Wisconsin State Journal reported Dennis Sieg was charged with "lying to a Dane County Judge and Sheriff's detective".

After I first retained Jim Cassidy to be my Attorney, he advised he recently had a client who committed suicide because his divorce hadn't gone well. He didn't give details, but I think I was beginning to find out why. What I was seeing was a circus of pomposity and billable activities, with a Judge seeming to favor my being fleeced by the Lawyers from the McManus Law firm. Some of the billable activities clearly included fraudulent appraisals, false and inflammatory declarations, and things I couldn't even understand. But, I could see I was financially important because I was the only one bleeding money.

- **A divorce trial, over a year after filing.**

The "Trial" proceedings are foggy memories whereby the Judge and Lawyers practiced their courtroom protocol, and charged at their increased "courtroom" rates. The trial was to provide testimony as to the factors to be considered in the divorce, e.g. health of each party, employment and employability, statements from each as to valuations for bank accounts, stocks, personal property, and the big dollar item - the house.

For fairness to be reached, it was important to cross examine the appraisers under oath to ask them why there was double counting of personal property, inconsistent valuations of the same items, to identify and correct erroneous calculations, and to discover how Mr. Stien arrived at an unimaginable house valuation that was 128% greater than my bank's valuation for refinancing or the Dane County Assessor's office fair market valuation. The 128% valuation inflated the amount of hypothetical equity in the house to almost three times of what could be realized, e.g. the mortgage amount would stay fixed with the exaggerated value all being declared to be equity. Yes, they had refused to let the house be sold.

Clever?

You can see why I had requested we sell the house and divide the actual proceeds. And you can see why others adversely said: "No!"

On the day of the "trial" all of the appraisers were available for cross-examination, but Judge Angela Bartell arbitrarily dismissed them without any cross-examinations. Thus the Judge precluded us from exposing any financial monkey business.

This has been explained to me to be within the discretionary authority of the court.

The appraisers went home and my Attorney was asked to attend a meeting with Anna's Attorney in Judge Bartell's chambers to discuss whatever it was I wasn't supposed to hear. In asking my Attorney as to what happened in the Judge's chambered meeting, my Attorney only said: "It could have been worse."

I suppose Judge Bartell might have also considered having me make alimony payments like forever and forever. The discretionary limits for a Family Court Judge do not seem to have any limits. So yes, I can imagine it could have been worse. But, I could also see how my Attorney had been intimidated into acquiescing without any chance to consult with me. I can only assume my Attorney acted in my best interest – as best as she could.

* **Judge A. Bartell issued a Memorandum Decision - On November 11, 1984**

Then came the Memorandum Decision so loaded with bogus numbers and mathematical magic it almost made me sick. It couldn't be true! Some of the exaggerated numbers were obvious, and the Judge had chosen the 128% house appraisal.

There was no evidence she even stopped to think about taking an average of my certified appraisals with the non-certified 128% appraisal for the house, or to average the figures for other items.

I recognized many funny numbers, but with all the smoke and mirrors I missed some of the twist and turns incorporated in the Judge's Memorandum Decision. My Attorney was familiar with the way the system worked and how the numbers were created. I didn't know how the court worked but I was assured by my Attorney the Judge could correct the "errors" (??) during the "Reconsiderations" phase of the divorce process.

Funny numbers and falsified appraisals are obviously old stuff for the eyes of a seasoned Judge, as carried into the Family Court by some divorce Attorneys. Although this might look like an organized racketeering system, the "You fleece this one, and I fleece the next one" system has been explained to me, by a knowledgeable Attorney, as allowable via the discretionary authority of the court.

These things can't happen without Judgeship support. We can explain the Lawyer things by following the money, but what about the Judges? What can the Judges get out of these deals? A sponsorship for a State of Wisconsin Supreme

Court Judgeship appointment, a re-election endorsement, a tip for a good real estate investment, or what? In any case I believe I was onto why Attorney Cassidy's previous client had committed suicide. The ordered payoff was almost three times more than what would seem to be a properly calculated amount. Hence, I was still hopeful for reconsideration of the list of items forwarded to the Judge for her attention.

I had actually thought some errors and the exaggerated house appraisal would be corrected – if for no other reason than there was no way I could ever get one-half of the specified amount of money together. One half of their specified total was more than our combined total for marital assets plus what I could borrow. I thought the Judge could see this and at least make some corrections to give me a plausible amount.

* **My requests for reconsiderations - 12/28/84**

My requests for reconsiderations, were:

** Excess valuations of my personal property and double counting. Valuations were up to double of what the same assessors gave me at the time of their assessment. Several items were listed in the final exhibits more than once.

** Under valuation of my non-marital interest.

** Excess valuation by entering a future value of retirement funds instead of a current value, as per exhibits, affidavit and Court exhibit #38. For example, $100,000 payable in 7 years has a present or current value of approximately $50,000 if discounted at 7.5%. Thus, a future value is an inflated present value. Family Court Judges and Lawyers know this. However, litigants may not be so clear about this difference and be bamboozled.

** Excess valuation of house at 128% of State of Wisconsin certified fair market value and Mid-America appraisals. This excessive valuation <u>more than doubles the amount of presumed equity.</u>

The above were clearly "done on purpose" mistakes. I thought everybody could see their mistakes (?) were so excessive there would be no way I could finance their call for a settlement. And yes, failure to pay would leave me in contempt of the Family Court order for payment. I felt sure Judge Bartell could see this and would make some adjustments so everything could work out okay.

But!

***After six months without any reconsideration I received a summons from the court calling for a Contempt of Court hearing for non-payment of the bogus property settlement - 7/8/85**

Yes, this was a court ordered demand for payment of a court specified amount of money (?). I would have gladly paid to the limit of my cash and loan ability and be done with it, but the court's payoff demand was over my head. In fact, there was enough information before the court and Attorneys that I could only believe they knew I wasn't going to be able to come up with the enhanced payoff amount. So what's their game? Put me in contempt of court? Send me to Jail? Embarrass me? Stress the patience of my employer?

I didn't mind there was a financial bias that favored Anna, but why push it so far as to trash me out, set me up for jail time and cause damage or loss of my employment? This over-kill could also make the divorce proceedings go on-and-on along with Lawyers fees. As for any employer, the U.S. Forest Service has little patience for this kind of employee trouble, and prefer to let the local authorities have their way. I was worried. All I did was to file for a divorce, and now this?

In the meantime, I was back in the house again, and Anna was back in California with her family. There was wear and tear, and minor damage to the house from the years Anna was left to be the sole occupant of the house. The first appraisal I came up with on the house for a loan was only 77% of the value Judge Bartell adopted. After making needed repairs and painting I was able to get an appraisal for 80% of Judge Bartell's value. This still wasn't enough. It looked like I was trapped with no way out.

There was no way I could get the money demanded, and I couldn't understand why our requests for reconsiderations were ignored. I was naive. I thought I could trust Judge Angela Bartell for fair consideration. I couldn't believe this was happening.

I took leave from work to meet with my Attorney for a Courthouse hearing with Court Commissioner Snyder. I was counting on this hearing to bring a remedy for the situation via a degree of reconsideration. But, at the hearing, Court Commissioner Snyder abruptly, like knowing what was going to come said he didn't have time to listen to why I couldn't come up with the money, and grumbled he would never have time to listen to any of my excuses. He dismissed the hearing with the warning that if I didn't come up with the payoff in one week I would be in contempt of court. (Contempt of court? Jail time?) I was given one week to appear with the money – or else?

Wow! I had tried, and I couldn't. My Attorney appeared to be as bewildered as I was. We know I can't come up with the money specified, so I'll be in contempt of court! Jail?

At that point I lost any hope that I might be rescued by way of any reconsiderations. That would probably mean I fork over every dollar I could get my hands on, and be saddled with a high interest IOU to cover a balance, plus a penalty, to be paid off in installments. Of course this would also mean I would remain under the watchful eye of the Family Court. I could see this could go on and on like forever and ever with more Attorney fees and intrusions into my place of work.

Why?

I've been told many times my story is "a dime a dozen" kind of Family Court story. So?

I worked at a Federal agency where our Personnel Officer told me it was their duty to cooperate with the local state and county authorities - without any questions. So the Federal Personnel Officer at my place of work was compromised, i.e. instructed to not interfere with or question these Family Court related activities. Thus, the Family Court Lawyers specifically requested summons servers to serve their court summons to people at their place of work. A couple of times servers came to where I was living and told me they refused to serve me at work saying they knew it was just a way for the Family Court Lawyers to harass a person.

Going into a person's workplace can tag you as someone to watch and gossip about, and maybe dig into you if given the chance. A religious zealot you may be working with may think this is their duty. No matter, your divorce is not a good thing to bring into your work place – for you or your employer. The Family Court practitioners know this, but ***do do*** it.

Work place intrusions by the Family Court can cost you your job. And how are you going to continue to keep paying all those people if you lose your job? Of course, you don't. You might even become homeless and hopeless before the Family Court gets done with you.

So help!

I was clearly insolvent and the Family Court Commissioner had me facing a contempt of court charge that could lead to jail time, more work place embarrassment, and corrosive employment effects. So, why not file for bankruptcy and bring some outsider's eyes in to see what's going on in the Family Court?

** I knew I couldn't get the money, so I filed for Bankruptcy Protection 8/6/85 (MM&-85-10516) to stay out of jail.

Bankruptcy worked marvelously. It was easy to fill the forms out that clearly showed I was bankrupt in accordance with all of the certified accounting and appraisal details I had. Most importantly, it disabled the Dane County Family Court from being able to find me in contempt of court for non-payment of their ransom and sending me to their jail. Thank God the bankruptcy stopped the wheels of injustice. However, Judge Angela Bartell immediately sent me a summons for a hearing, whereby the Bankruptcy Court considerately assigned a Lawyer to be with me to guarantee my bankruptcy protection. When asked, I testified to Judge Bartell what had occurred during Court Commissioner Snyder's last hearing, e.g. he said he didn't think he would ever have time to hear my excuses and threatened a contempt of court citation. Judge Bartell quickly told the clerk to strike my testimony from the record. I wondered why? Why would the Family Court Judge want to sweep my statement as to why I filed for bankruptcy under the carpet?

* **Discharge of Debtor - 12/17/86**

The Bankruptcy court made distributions to my list of creditors, including a payment of $3,445.00 to Anna – a fraction of the amount prescribed by Judge Bartell, but considered fair by the bankruptcy court.

* **What happened to the Reconsiderations that could have avoided the Bankruptcy??**

A request for Reconsiderations was initially submitted to Judge Angela Bartell on December 28, 1984. Then the weeks and months rolled by. There was never any evidence Judge Bartell was going to reconsider anything. I began thinking the Dane County Court System had betrayed me, and might be responsible for a lot of Machiavellian murders, i.e. Family Court related suicides. But I don't think people want to know what our Family Courts are able to quietly do, or to be concerned about their divorce related suicides, e.g. it's unbelieveable.

At this point I began to see the evil wisdom of Judge Angela Bartell's sheltering of the exaggerated appraisal of the house and items of personal property, and why she denied me the option to sell the house for a fair market value. Thus my trust in Wisconsin's Dane County Family Court system began to fail.

Judge Bartell issued a memorandum on May 5, 1986. On page 4 of this document, the first paragraph reads:

"The petitioner has filed extensive motions for reconsideration dated October 4, 1985 and the court concludes that most of the arguments made by petitioner were not made at trial and therefore cannot be considered. Accordingly, petitioner's motions for reconsideration are denied."

Her predication is a flat out lie! It was the Judge who specifically dismissed the appraisers from their presence at the trial, i.e. they were there for examination and sent home by the Judge.

My faith in this combination of Family Court Judgeship, Lawyers, and "rules of law" went out the window.

At her discretion, Judge Bartell **refused** to hear testimony by way of the cross-examination of appraisers at trial. So she now lies and ignores the 12/28/84 request for reconsiderations, and refused to average the appraisals. Any one of which actions could have put the final settlement within my financial reach. So, "Shame on you Judge Angela Bartell." I think you deliberately cheated me to put me in a position where I could be in contempt of court. I think you are a street-wise Judge and know exactly what you are doing - sadistically. Why else? How can you make any money off of this kind of action?

As suggested by other authors, un-just actions and corruption cannot flourish without a given authority, a monopoly, and a lack of transparency – like what we find in our Family Court systems

* A contempt order and a Jail sentence from Judge Angela Bartell - 4/15/87

As previously mentioned, the McManus Lawyers always asked the sheriff selected to serve their court summons upon me at work, i.e. at the USDA Forest Service's Forest Products Laboratory. They must then appear at the front desk, identify themselves and announce their purpose for whom they want to contact. This then becomes a work place kind of announcement. As previously indicated, the summons server can choose to serve you at home. This time, however, the order arrived at my place of work by a direct order from Judge Angela Bartell!

Yes, the Judge is an attractive woman and has a nice smile. It's hard to look at her and not like her, but by this action I suddenly had a different picture of her and wondered if she was also the Judge for Attorney Cassidy's previous client who committed suicide? Were there others?

The order delivered to me at my place of work <u>by Judge Bartell's order</u>, read:

"IT IS HEREBY ORDERED that the Petitioner, George B. Harpole, is found in contempt of court for failure to make maintenance payments pursuant to the final judgment in the above captioned divorce action. (Supposedly discharged by bankruptcy?) It is further ordered that the Petitioner shall be sentenced to six months in the Dane County Jail for said contempt. However, the Petitioner may purge himself of said jail sentence by commencing maintenance payments in the total amount of $350.00 every two weeks on April 10, 1987, said payment reflecting $250.00 in maintenance and $100.00 toward existing arrearages." (Note: These are 1985 values taking significant percentages from my paycheck.)

"It is further ordered that a wage assignment shall be implemented forthwith with the Petitioner's employer, the U.S.D.A. Forest Service, Forest Products Laboratory, 1 Gifford Pinchot Drive, Madison, Wisconsin - 53703."

That's that! My Attorney said I could appeal. The rule of law appeared to be on my side, but with an appeal there would be no end in sight, and Attorney fees and court related distractions could go on-and-on. This was their ball park, not mine.

Extortion? So be it.

Hence, I begged to borrow what I needed to pay for my ransom. Some good friends also helped. I finally got it together and paid it off (11/16/87). One of the lending bankers wrote to tell me I had some really good friends who had helped me out. I was thinking those somebody's might have helped me out politically too. After all, it was rumored Judge Bartell was hoping for an appointment to the Wisconsin Supreme Court (she didn't make it). These things can have political aspects too.

On January 26, 1988 Judge Bartell issued an order announcing the termination of separate maintenance and the settlement of arrearages - ignoring the Federal Bankruptcy Court's discharge of debt. But bringing the Federal Bankruptcy Court into the game did help by pulling the blankets off of the Family Court, letting fresh eyes see what was going on, and surely keeping me from being found in contempt of court and going to a debtor's jail. So after 5 years of nonsense, this was final closure. But the stigma from those 5 years was toxic for my employment at the FPL. The FPL Director closed my section for Economic research.

I think the Family Court's actions had something to do with this turn in my employment status.

I was able to stay on the payroll for a diminished position but elected to leave after being advised I was to be transferred to another location. I felt this was a kind of excommunication from the FPL where I had worked for 17 years. So I elected to retire at the end of 1989 and move to Colorado to provide consulting services for forest management and conservation projects (Mesa Consulting). This was a good move – away from the threat and influence of the Dane County Family Court system.

Significances

Statistics from the Federal Center for Disease Control (CDC) indicate that out of approximately 30,000 suicides per year in the 1990's close to 15,000 of those suicides were being committed by men between the ages of 25 and 55, as opposed to 4,000 per year for women. One analyst estimated that during the 1990's approximately 14,850 suicides were committed each year specifically by divorced and separated men (antimisandry.com) - not counting those in the process of a divorce. Also, studies by Dr. Augustine J. Kposowa, Department of Sociology, University of California at Riverside, point to the same statistical conclusions.

Current statistics from our Center for Disease Control (CDC) indicate our national suicides of 30,622 for the year 2001 increased to 41,149 in 2013, with suicides among those from ages 35 to 64 increasing nearly 30% since 1999. Male suicides continued to be 4 times more frequent than for women[1,2], and perhaps related to the bias and bullying authority given to our Family Courts[3].

If you look at the figures like I have you might think I'm making a mountain out of an anthill. After all, there are around two million marriages in the U.S. each year (2014) offset by about one million divorces. That gives us 2-million divorced people each year with say 15,000 suicides. So we might say divorce related suicides probably kill less than 1% (~0.75%) of those who go through a divorce. From a Darwinian standpoint we might think of these suicides as a kind of genetic purification process. But, creating these distressed people may also create some recruiting targets for roaming terrorist, or simply increase the numbers of our jobless and homeless populations.

Besides an estimated 44.6-billion dollar a year medical and work loss costs associated with our annual suicide toll there are also serious economic costs connected to our homeless populations.[1]

We might like to take a closer look.

Homelessness

The number of divorce related suicides appear only as the tip of an iceberg – a fraction of the familial and one-person disasters that might be avoided if we had a more exposed and sensitive Family Court system. Shortly before setting himself on fire Tom Ball wrote lucidly on the subjects of overzealous enforcements of domestic violence laws and how they have led so many families into social and financial chaos, and homelessness.[5,8]

The starting point for familial disasters often begin when a husband and father thinks of himself as the head of his household, and feels a need to emphasize some perceived family

need seemingly important enough to be emphasized by way of a minor act or threat of violence. Thus, a mandatory arrest can be made even when there is no injury.

His wife or mother of his children – who decides to challenge his familial authority, takes the next step. She calls the local police who are typically told to make a "mandatory arrest" in the name of curbing  domestic violence – primarily as against women and children. Police Officers often have some discretionary authority, like whether to write a traffic ticket or a warning, but typically depending on the policies of their supervisors.

For example, check the Internet coverage regarding the plight of Adrian Peterson (NFL football player) who used a switch to discipline his 4-year-old boy. See what you think. At the bottom of the so called "mandatory" police actions seems to be the thought  credited to a writer of long ago, i.e. William Congreve (1670-1729) who is quoted as saying "Hell hath no fury like a woman scorned." What Adrian Peterson seems to have survived started from a complaint filed by the estranged mother of his 4-year old boy. Tom Ball's story is not very different, but after 10 years of Family Court control he decided to put an end to it all - to suicide. I call Tom Ball's death a Machiavellian murder.[3,4,5] In contrast, Adrian Peterson was cleared and forgiven for any wrongdoing, and was allowed back on the payroll of his NFL football team.

Tom Ball seemed to have been an ordinary guy, graduating from high school, going on to get a 4-year college degree, serving 21-years in the Army, was married, had 3 children and held a good job as a Customer Service person at a car dealership. Then, Tom Ball, maybe tainted by a PTSD from his 21-years of military experiences, had a minor child care event that esculated under the authorities of his local police and Family Court into a 10 year ordeal of supression, control, job loss, alienation, desperation; and, to finally end it all by suicide on the courthouse steps that led to the powers that conquered him – socially, spiritually and financially. Tom Ball's last words are as follows:

> "*Appareently the old general was right. Death is not the worst of evil. I am due in court the end of the month. The ex-wife's Lawyer wants me jailed for back child*

support. The amount ranges from $2,200 to $3,000 depending on who you ask. Not big money after being separated over ten years and unemployed for the last two. But I do owe it. If I show up for court without the money and the Lawyer says jail, then the judge will have the bailiff take me into custody. There really are no suprises on how the system works once you know how it actually works. And it does not work anything like they taught you in high school history or civics class. I could have made a phone call or two and borrowed the money, but <u>I am done being bullied</u> for being a man."

You can find the full text of Tom Ball's ~11,000-word statement on the Internet.[5] Much of his writing is extreme and not rational, but a lot of it checks out to be well considered and sufficiently accurate to justify presenting, to help explain where some of the causes for homelessness and hopelessness come from. For truthfulness I am mindful that Tom Ball is just steps away from dousing himself with gasoline and setting himself on fire – to die on the courthouse steps leading to where he was brought down to be totally defeated. So if you read his full statement you will be reading and feeling what it's like to be at the point of frustration and hopelessness where suicide becomes a viable alternative. From my own Family Court experience, I know how unfairness can create this kind of thinking.

Dear God, and to the powers that be, please save us from Tom Ball's experience.

Tom Ball passed along his findings with regard to the Law Enforcement and Family Court's discretionary protocols (not laws) that appear to be sending many to join our large populations of homeless men, women and children. At the root of the problem seems to be a "Mandatory Arrest" protocol practiced to discourage domestic violence – even when there is no physical harm to report. For whatever reason, the "Mandatory Arrest" protocol requires the culprit to be handcuffed, removed from the family household, and booked for a hearing by a Judge in the Family Court system. For many this leads to the loss of employment, and often times to eventual homelessness for the entire family. Remember, Tom Ball was arrested and removed from his home for slapping his 4-year-old daughter. The following are some excerpts from Tom Ball's writings:

"I was 48 years old when I got arrested here for my first time. So I went looking for the arrest numbers for domestic violence, this new group that I had unwilling joined. I could not find anything so I wrote the U.S. Dept. of Justice in Washington. They wrote back that they did not keep track of domestic violence arrests. The FBI keeps track of all other crimes. How come not domestic violence?

"The first thing I found was a study not of domestic violence arrests but of domestic violence injuries for 18 unnamed states and the D.C. in the year 2000. In the study 51% of the injuries were 'no injuries,' so I knew I had a study of police reports. Who else but a police officer would record 'no injuries'? I populated that out to 50 states and came up with 874,000 arrests for the year 2000."

Tom Ball then made estimates of the accumulated number of "mandatory arrests" that might have been made starting back in 1984. He then writes:

"The number I have now in 2011 is 36 million adults have been arrested for domestic violence. I have a gut feeling this number could be as high as 55 million, but

I only have data to 36 million. So 36 million it stays. And there is a really cool trick you can do once you have this number. You can find out how many American men, women and children ended up homeless because of these arrests.

"Most of the domestic violence statistics I have seen break down with 75% male and 25% female being arrested.

"Child support is usually 33% of the man's gross income. Withholding for taxes, social security and health insurance can range up to 28% of his gross paycheck. So a man making $500 a week gross has only $825 monthly left over after withholding and child support. That is not enough money for an apartment here in Central Massachusetts. That does not include other expenses like heating, electric, gas, groceries, telephone, cable, car payment and car insurance. So he is in a financial hole. Estimates of homeless men run 82% to 94%. I am going to round that down to 80%.

"His wife runs into a problem. She was getting his whole paycheck for the household. Now she gets a third for child support. Figure they both work and made *the same money, her budget went from 100% down to 66%. If she was running the house on $3,045 a month when the King was home, now without him, she only has $2,220. Most households in America cannot withstand a 27% hit on the household account. She'll juggle the bills but eventually most wives figure out that they can pay all the smaller bills if they just do not pay the big bill. That would be the rent or the mortgage. So six to nine months after the King is out of the castle, the Queen, the Princes and the Princesses are also on the street. Domestic violence feminists state that 50% of victim spouses of domestic violence end up homeless at some time in their lives.*

"The last groups of homeless from these arrests are children. The domestic violence feminists state that 70% of domestic violence couples have children. So 50% female times 70% children equals 35%. But children are plural. So we will double that to 70%.

Tom Ball's conclusion is that there have been *"72 million men, women and children ending up homeless at some point in their lives over the last 25 years because of the 'mandatory arrest' protocol practiced by local police and enforced by our Family Court services."*

So Tom Ball's figures suggest almost 2-million men, women and children become newly categorized as homeless each year – due to the protocols enforced by many  burrows of police and Family Court systems. And, what about the abandonment effects on those too young to understand – like what happened to my wife Marta?

So, is a family unit worth saving? Should the Family Court's influence be considered in the events of suicides and homelessness? Are drug use, depression and other mental illnesses causes for, or are they the results of becoming homeless?

So who cares?

Albert Einstein wrote: "The world is a dangerous place to live; not because of the people who are evil, but because of the people who don't do anything about it."

A Program for Change

I think the following 7 changes would help neutralize the worst of the evil activities sheltered by our Family Court systems. See what you think:

#1. Our Family Courts would not be allowed to incarcerate anyone and be limited to "Contempt of Court" fines not to accumulatively exceed $500; whereafter petitioners would either be referred to an arbitration panel or provided a change of Judgeship.

#2. It should be unlawful for anyone with Family Court authority to contact or cause another to contact a person's place of employment or business for Family Court purposes other than for wage garnishments.

#3. Every person with Family Court authority should be issued a suicide scorecard and not be protected from civil or criminal prosecutions for being an accessory to a suicide or murder.

#4. Adversarial practices would not be tolerated for Family Court actions. An arbitration panel should be engaged for the resolution of arguable differences and not be left to the discretion of a residing judge.

#5. Domestic abuse should not be a Family Court concern. And squabbles and verbal abuse complaints should not concern the Family Court. However, Family Court proceedings must be suspended until any criminal assault charges for physical abuse are resolved, i.e. where class II or greater levels of physical injury are evident and thereby justify criminal assault charges.

#6. Require every Coroner's inquest for a suicide to identify any presence or influence of a Family Court proceeding upon a victim's election to suicide.

#7. Require every Family Court Judge and Coroner in the United States to have a copy of this booklet.

A seven-step program. Okay?

References

1. Center for Disease Control and Prevention (CDC) (Internet). Feb 16, 2016. <u>Deaths: Final Data for 2013</u>. National Vital Statistics Report, Vol. 64, No.2.

2. CDC (Internet). May 3, 2013. <u>Suicide among adults aged 35–64 years—United States, 1999–2010</u>. Morbidity and Mortality Weekly Report, vol.62/No17.

3. CDC (Internet). 2014. <u>The Relationship Between Bullying and Suicide</u>. CDC Adobe PDF library.

4. Machiavelli, Nicolo. 1513. <u>The Prince.</u> Publisher: CreateSpace, Nov. 29, 2014. 82pp.

5. The Sentinel (internet). June 16, 2011. <u>Last Statement sent to Sentinel from Self-immolation Victim</u>. (Tom Ball's last statement.)

6. Sorge, Joseph and James Scurlock. 2014. <u>Divorce Corp</u>. 221pp

7. Sorge, Joseph. 2014. <u>Divorce Corp</u>. DVD, 1-hr 33-min

8. Wickipedia (Internet). Feb. 2015. Homelessness in The United States.

A Family Forever

Together or Apart

www.ingramcontent.com/pod-product-compliance
Lightning Source LLC
Chambersburg PA
CBHW071525180526
45171CB00002B/382